Free Verse Editions

Edited by Jon Thompson

THE REPUBLIC OF SONG

Kelvin Corcoran

Parlor Press
Anderson, South Carolina
www.parlorpress.com

Parlor Press LLC, Anderson, South Carolina, 29621

Printed in the United States of America
S A N: 2 5 4 - 8 8 7 9

Library of Congress Cataloging-in-Publication Data on File

978-1-64317-169-2 (paperback)
978-1-64317-170-8 (PDF)
978-1-64317-171-5 (ePUb)

1 2 3 4 5

Cover design by John Hall.

Parlor Press, LLC is an independent publisher of scholarly and
trade titles in print and multimedia formats. This book is available
in paperback and ebook formats from Parlor Press on the World
Wide Web at http://www.parlorpress.com or through online and
brick-and-mortar bookstores. For submission information or to
find out about Parlor Press publications, write to Parlor Press,
3015 Brackenberry Drive, Anderson, South Carolina, 29621, or
email editor@parlorpress.com.

CONTENTS

The Republic of Song

TO WRITE A MYTH OLOGY

RUE DES HIBOUX

1

To write a mythology
        commensurate to an ignorant island
        is not difficult.
They were of that class of traitor
self-serving, unimaginative.

Their only skill
        to make the poor vote for poverty
        the preterite for abandonment.
Oh bury me quietly
        in Hardy's field.

*

I perch my head in a bare room
on Rue des Hiboux, dogs bark in French
Ash and Silver Birch talk all night.

Reynard at the rubbish
on the tree-darkened road
Europe at the corner.

His delicate step, his nose in filth
by comparison is noble
and not given to self-destruction.

*

- What in the shape of a cloud?
A cloud in the shape of a cloud
in the shape of an imagined country
adrift on the edge of a continent.

- Doubtful, we've moved on from that,
  since meteorology usurped portents.
It disintegrates anyway, thin as air
snagged on a fault mid-Atlantic.

I like the high ones up there,
silver white capsules full of people
sun under their wings gliding the trade routes
rising to the world, the many.

2

To drill a hole in this wall is hard,
you need an extra-long bit to get through the granite
but then, task accomplished, you can pack in the charge
play the fool and bring the house down.

As if I might say – Jerusalem is fallen, lie down and weep;
a blunt truth, as if you might hear high-toned counterpoint
spinning in the eaves a social contract of forgotten triumph
turned to spite and Albion absurd.

3

Ironies are everywhere like roadworks on the pavement
and although I might not find the Supermarché,
my short-term memory shot, my sense of direction set at zero,
is as nothing compared to that country called England.

There the fields sing no more, the road taken buried in connivance
and time runs backwards to an empire of amnesia.
What is the name for the shade of green where the holloway leads,
where they travelled to follow the trade of their day?

Yes - the high ones up there zip zip like silver bullets,
there's a silver bullet and there are flightpaths above us,
they form and evaporate as we pass, there's a silver bullet,
the ones I like over the cities of Europe light the sky.

Biographies of the Brexiteers

The Quiet Man

Iain Guido Smith did make division and gather the spoils
plied his bonny craft the Centre for Social Justice far,
tacking across the lake of fire all the way to Betsygate.

Then setting fires in Baghdad and Washington and London,
his smug little face caressed by the claw of the Lady Margaret,
he conspired in the smoky arts of a sovereign nation once again.

The image which must enter through the image deserted him
his stand-up was only comical when he tried for gravitas
his mirage bucket for storing mirage history had a fuck hole in it.

As the girl Europa struggled all at sea, Guido looked on dreaming,
arranged the limbs of the drowned to spell Breakthrough Britain;
and gathered the spoils to build a new nation for old time's sake.

*

Twisting Michael of the Gove

The king sat in fair Witney Town
drinking the casual wine:
*Where can I find a good true knight
to keep the land for this clan of mine?*

I will, said the Gove, *trust me,*
said Michael of the shifty border
with betrayal in his shrivelled heart,
the Gove across the water.

You must call me minister
of speed-speak abjuring thought
and I will lead you backwards
into an England of last resort.

He turned his coat again again
sporting repugnant on either side
a dark and double lie disclosed;
Follow me follow me, he cried.

A loud laugh laughed he
in a future fifty fathoms deep,
there lies the bad Michael
with the nation at his feet.

*

Boris Johnson and *Seventy Two Virgins*

I imagined there was a prime minister
and that he had written a comic novel
and it was called Seventy Two Clichés;
a pile of stercus polished with huff-puff rags
which disclosed a steaming mind-set
at home in the ruling class for decades.

Cameron is an American research assistant,
she is a beautiful woman and available;
the British police are bumbling but kind;
the BBC is run by cunning liberal cowards;
and the main character, resembling the author,
ah, yes, right, bumbled into a leading role.

A fake Asian TV crew English flummery
the gun bucked a gargoyle's shoulder
the House of Sharmoota kingly lineage
a sharpshooter, Dean, Habib and Haroun
and spiteful Debbie from The Daily Mirror:
reconstruct the nonsense for yourself.

*'Dog-fuckers and corpse-eaters and gloom-addicts rule the future
with excrement.'*

—Odysseus Elytis, *The Axion Esti,*
translated by Edmund Keely and George Savidis

RADIO LOGOS

1

Should I dance on the mouth music scales?
Meaning nothing, meaning valve dust.
Why taunt the dumb beast?

Well, this aside, you must listen to my morning broadcast
I've recharged the arcane batteries of Radio Logos
stroked the air and rewired the marvels of Hellas.

Do you like that tone? A little grandiose for you?
Certainly not a song bird in a cage eating its own droppings.
Lesson 1: don't be a hired mouth or pundit.

Lesson 2: you must remember only archaeology is true:
the invention of sailing, recall the beauty of trade routes
but the meaning of unread inscriptions can change everything.

Good: the valves are humming and the meters flicker,
the dust burns, I tap tap the microphone – you can hear me,
you can hear these words remade on waves of morning air.

2

Has the colour of the sea broken your heart yet,
the air in blue waves transformed your seeing,
the bronze mountains turned your head? Yes?

So there's hope for you then, listen. – Lesson 3:
There is no history that does not relate to the present,

we know this, we know the cities that once were mighty etc.

They're nothing now but decrepit dormitories
populated by the insular, the ignorant;
imagine a country shrinking into itself: terminal.

The meaning of an unread binary choice
has changed everything, a future unexamined;
picture an island slowly rowing to the America.

The Tinny Islands go trumpety-trump
and sink in a fog of self-absorption
as the princes pipe their old new tunes.

3

I sit here on the edge of time gazing out to sea;
if history is an account of semantic drift
it can be read backwards to the well of speaking.

That was lesson 4 – were you even listening?
Were you just smiling at the pretty dial-light?
So here it is again – call it Terms of Resistance.

Lesson 4: you must trust the people, their erudition
from unlikely sources, from the stream of first meaning
from the mouths of all the people under the ringing sky.

As surprising as the beauty of recalled trade routes
the acquisition of obsidian, highland cedar and coral,
the expansion of ritual activity, the invention of sailing.

As surprising as the small pool of cool water
found high in the mountains, that bright ellipse
keeping a cold eye on the arching blue.

4

Their country has played itself out,
Eng-a-land has played itself out;
I landed there, loaded with memory.

It was a novelty dog show in the spring,
the sun made arrows of every blade of grass
the hills folded into themselves a miracle of green.

And here they come, the happy dog lovers
in their camper vans, Freedom, Odyssey, Rambler,
grinning and panting like dogs to a tilted field.

At the close they dive into a sclerotic sea,
buried under a regular sunset, hardly making a splash,
taking the living with them: thanatocracy.

Your country has played itself out,
no those feet did not – Freedom, Odyssey, Rambler;
this is the anti-Jerusalem.

MR PRESIDENT'S NEW HAT

'Genghis Khan loves his new mauve hat'
(Genghis Khan's hat. Lee Harwood)

Mr President loves his new red hat;
go rally beyond its spinning shadow,
hear the music, see the pictures
and dance one step across the sea.

Shostakovich set light to Brussels that night
and the young cellist flew up to the ceiling.
I went six times to the Bruegel show,
saw good Doctor Williams and dreamt of Europe.

Red cap rolls across the border down Sonora way,
snagged on a prickly pear the desert does its business
and the original legend is folded back and sullied,
tattooed with sand ake arica eat aga.

By train to The Hague across the flatlands
open stretches of water like a second sky,
the masters of light are waiting in line,
to be as in life but with symbols displayed.

Young women look out from lavish interiors,
indicate oysters, a bowl of onions, red roses,
and she's there, that girl turning, a pearl,
a gaze as still as a sky of reflected water.

Red cap rolls on further south and all around is desert
and the desert of ideas; a jack rabbit takes a bite
k am t ga a distracted coyote anoints a claim
red cap yellowed comes to rest with bleached trash.

The point is an ordinary day before us
and the landscape of just what happens,
a city stands off in the painted distance
the ploughman's bent shoulders deny tragedy.

The dog attends, the shepherd looks away,
a wind fills the sail and Icarus kicks the sea;
a dead man feeds the root of thought
and there's ploughing to be done.

> *Scorpion takes refuge in the engorged and tattered dome*
> *at aga ma all around lamentation sounds in darkness;*
> *empty red cap with flaccid peak dreams am ic gr e*
> *venomous and stealthy predators innocent by comparison.*

The Near Distance

Now that I've recovered from the time of flat vision
all things do stack up in a way, for instance the clouds
above the moving trees behind the apartments opposite.

The ambition to make depth from the single plane returns,
unconfined by the immediate intricacy of leaf mosaic,
as if seeing hovers above the wet gardens and engulfed houses.

The vision machine runs in the heart of this civilisation
issues revelations, battlefields, boys in mud arranged in choirs
fly over Maastricht to circle the open city of Cologne.

To have regained the pleasure of layered vision unbound,
to have blood flow to those parts of the brain unrestricted,
means learning to see again out of a blank, blind zero.

There are suburban conifers here receding into the near distance,
closer, a silver birch, then a bank of deciduous trees I can't name,
staged alongside a raised road of a hedge under an open sky.

Light plays variously, turning the pale underside of leaves
as the wind moves everything together and apart,
the windows of seeing open and close in the shadowed transepts.

Conifers, silver birch, a young ash tree inclined, already there,
the full spectrum cast across the fields of Europe, the circuits of
history;
risen light exacting every blade of grass, every recalled name.

THE WHITE ROAD

If I went back there would I hear her voice
and see those figures again, that side of the family
the other side of time folded in the blue and green hills
of the Slad Valley as evening falls under luminous distance
and they work out their lives, come and go,
turn that field to better use, raise children, stop?

There's a patch of light in the sky seems to pause
and shed a painterly quality on common nativity
picturing the practical, hard-bitten characters,
raising the fallen as if still walking long-legged
over hedges, brimming ditches, taking the road to town
with the blue green valley at their backs alight.
I see them come tramping over the fields,
catch the rough old songs beating in their hearts.

*

The boy dreamt of a white road,
night was all around but the white road shone;
he walked along it thinking it was death
and everything said – no invention is allowed.

Poetry was buried in the mud and muck of the ditch,
he forgot its sound and wondered if it ever happened;
the black trees bore the names of the all the girls he'd known
and the spaces between the things making sense enlarged.

I would rather walk in the Atlantic light of Penwith,
the tilting perspective painted by Ben Nicholson
spilling us east and west into the slapping sea
as we teeter on Celtic fields, skate on granite hedges.

Day recalls that village to the left of the lane,
a bridge of sorts over the pell-mell stream and its aria.

*

In Europe now, in our city garden,
bats jinx the trees as the light goes
and we sit and talk and talk;
here you are, bright one in darkness.
I can lay out memories like a dance
the days the girls were born
you standing there in a lit doorway
and we walked into a new world.

The silver flightpaths flash above us,
arrival departure, arrival departure;
at the end of the garden is the unknown
and there's no talking there;
only chemistry counts, words fail
walking the damp steps underground.

THE SINKING COLONY REVISITED IN THE DAYS OF LEE HARWOOD

A trail of bookmarks, a trail of postcards
I found around the house after you left
tic-tac-toe through the little labyrinth
a string of shining beads in a lost currency
and many different faces came and went
in the days of the days of Lee Harwood.

Poet most alive living nowhere now
clues come fluttering from the shelves,
late arrivals from not the full story,
that walk we never made across the Downs
Grasscut CD 1 inch ½ mile, map and voices
drilling holes in the discontinued calendar.

*

This was all so but from another time
the reminders kept arriving, the paths not taken beckoned,
that secluded bay in the heat of the afternoon
after the rains finished and a translucent curtain opened
across the whole vista of their other ways.

And though the scheme was for the benefit of all,
the metropolis and the dominions let's say,
there was a groundswell and unexpected events;
the radicalisation of the tennis club,
the close down of the baking circle,
the preference for autochthonic dance.

Your soft linen like a wing swept the veranda
analogous to the mystery of the rain-washed view,
another season of calculations, of glad-handing
the nabobs and salesmen, their butterfly wives.

At least the women set the air alight, a sort of flagrance
I never knew if it was sex or absent-mindedness,
lost deep in the intricacies of the local dialect
itself a version of an implacable, closed book,
it might as well have been shapes scratched on rock
or pitter-patter feet around the bay for all I grasped,
I just never knew and none of us saw it coming;
I like to think our expeditions were genuine,
were not always for cover but for pure geology.

Later I learnt Captain Harwood's reports were correct,
they predicted the whole thing – you just couldn't tell,
he was so unassuming, gentle in his detachments,
and the reports were filed in Government House,
under a heading of Fanciful Imaginings At Large.

I suppose the engine of the age can run on,
can drive every detail of our lives and loyalties
and we don't talk about it, we just don't see it
and I came to think that's because we're inside it
encompassed and blind, duty-bound, modern.

I still thought this when she left for England,
that she had failed, fallen into a character flaw,
and I lay there every night under vague imaginings
pretty ghosts circling the mosquito net, entwined
low susurrations of an erotic folk literature
released from their red mouths all night.

I must close, be done, you have been very patient,
there's no final account and the inventory continues,
a delivery of leather buckets for the collection of Yak milk,
wrongly dispatched, bullets of incorrect calibre,
non-regulation dubbing, polo mallets and hegemony cranks.

All I can do is wait for the cargo boat to arrive
let it edge its way into the bay without reprisal,
I doubt they even know the name of this place.

*

Trail of postcards to nowhere then, unaddressed
straight through the winding Platonic streets;
England crouches, its back turned on Europe
resentful, effaces history and dreams an America;
despite this you can see the sea from Brunswick Place
and poetry leaps at the high windows there,
you meet an old friend go to a bar and the stars appear.

Take the scenes connected over the years in turn,
each one designed by Donald Evans open, unresolved:
poet and old friend, the years relived in one night;
poet tackles bank robber, receives public acclaim;
poet in a foreign city at one, making himself at home;
poet in labyrinth turns, follows the sound of the sea;
poet scales the final mountain, everyone's there, it's ok.

THE REPUBLIC OF SONG

COME UP COME UP

At night I think of the living and the dead
the Irish songs rise like light over Carrickfergus
and I lose my way on Grafton Street,
heading out for the Republic of Song.

In the Republic of Song we're all walking,
I see my father on the road from Wexford Town;
he survives the war and beats the drink,
I see him now on the black road turnabout.

*

Andy, let's walk along the cliffs, the turfy paths and rocks,
step high across the rumours, the old epiphanies spent,
and fling the whole lot into the uncased Atlantic air
with the Spring-dizzy fauna and every thought of art.

The raptor, the drone, the water streaming from the hill;
let all the music of earth figure by turns the path we walk;
let the Victor Freeman, twenty miles off Wolf Rock,
return safely to harbour and the sea settle its speech in the wake.

We saw Lee set off westward over the unlikely blue wave;
mountaineer, poet, friend, restored to all tenderness,
the good man Harwood, not waiting on pastoral rhapsody,
sees everything; the history of dead men singing underground,
the quick green one-time flash of the darting lizard
and the roll of the land overflowing to the final sea.

*

A History of the World in Twelve Maps
complete with a postcard from Lee;
2008, *I'm setting out on a new stage*
and this summer he's a year dead.

From the *oikumene* to map the whole world,
from the body to the hearth to the horizon;
the outer salt-sea's no province for the living
though we walked the shoreline from your door.

The moon has made the sea milky,
opaque the memory of our commonweal,
that lost country where we once followed
a different life in the nation of now.

*

Spring landed in the small garden Brussels,
the day lost to Roy – and a glass of wine;
all the creatures go at it again, the fox stares,
various insects and assorted birds
glide their songs on the turning air.

Listen hard to the name they speak,
a dancing trio of notes – Roy Fisher, Roy Fisher;
there's a green plot, a thinking shade
where that hare, zig-zagging slowly
imprints its paw on poetry's field-path.

Roy read as he wrote with no show, no pomp;
in Newcastle-under-Lyme twenty years ago
standing with Carl Rakosi and Gael Turnbull:
come up, come up my thinking shades,
see that hare *zig-zagging slowly like the shadow of a hare.*

*

I thought I saw Robert Sheppard in the market
Place Dumon, Brussels, bright for business
wearing a leather fedora and a fine jacket,
looking for the language of the language of poetry.

He was smiling at the Coquilles St-Jacques,
smelling the hot waffles on the morning air:
Robert Robert, what do you have there?
- Ah yes, well, I've an appetite for all these things
  and I'm thinking about Lee Harwood.

But Lee's a ghost now, a nothing, a film
turning uncast on the day, a thought
of the shadow platforms for the dancing trees
standing out like visions across the Downs
where the light infiltrates their leaves
for Spring in another country.

*

In the Republic of Song we're all walking
and you see us now on the black road turnabout.

GRAHAMLAND

The house where Graham lived
in Madron in the rain
is a shell of song to a light tenor
longing for Loch Thom.

Next door on Mount View Terrace
a satellite dish suspended
listens to the running streams
make ready the risen speech.

From his house of granite, house of words
the moor is flying blind
the black lane shining at the sky
for Penwith to silence babble.

The granite spiral staircase
from the Madron workhouse refit
lies broken up and buried
in the fields of Grahamland.

Treads worn smooth by the feet of the poor
ascending and descending
in the fields of Grahamland
where poetry takes its turn.

*

The second location of Grahamland can be found
at S 65° W 63°, country code AQ, population zero,
though names are disputed it's there, waiting for your step.

Using dog sleds and a de Havilland Fox Moth
we determined that Grahamland was a peninsula,
a white tenement in an unfixed magnetic field

Half-seen through the interference of the snow;
then the snow becomes the fabric of your breathing
and you hear high voices on the other side of blizzard.

The worst of it was settling down at night alone,
the ice song sounding from the deep sea channels
sets the world atilt roaring at the broken door.

*

The last of Grahamland, *listen back, listen back,*
is the white tenement of memory and bare language,
the worst of it how the uninhabited names weather
- and this on a day of talk in the green wood of Madron.

And that would be the Graham Reel you join,
as if there ever was a choice, as the brimming tide
breaks in particles belonging as first light on Fore Street
launched even later there becoming a time.

- Do you know a poet called W S Graham lived here?
Yes, I do, there's a plaque up there on the wall – look.
See the day showing its colours, swaying to the sky
and see that large body of water sounding us out.

Launched even later there becoming a time.

MESSAGES COMING IN

Glenn Gould arrived today in the arms of J S Bach,
from the garden of morning the aria zoomed
over the sun –cracked quay and inclined greenery.
Roger Hilton back flipped a perfect arc – *Get me out of here.*
Where's my bloody boat and which way is the Cote d'Azur?

The advocates of Spring dig the spreading mulch,
dig the mud, the tubers, the building block sequence
to find the roots of ascendency;
at the edge of the turning world sweet mouth
proclaiming delight in unlike forms.

His fingers in the soil, at first chthonic cold
rise to blood temperature to find the literal,
the sounds of the world entering all around;
these floating bodies transduced take shape
by efflorescence, by intelligence, by flight.

BN

This is the Atlantic-washed radiant town
drenched in that light imagined again on the side of life.

In this way Ben Nicholson returned vision to the world,
that such things could be made from seeing.

In this unfixed landscape perceptual certainty is challenged
and you wake dousing your head in the western approaches.

In the arrangement of these shapes, these colours, this whiteness
pleasure is a sort of common sense of light and its geometry.

There you can totter all day on an inverted luminous bowl
augment the brimming world in the various planes of seeing.

Imagined again in Ticino, Paros and Rievaulx,
the pencil draws and carves, the stylus draws and carves.

Working through to the primer, to chase out something alive.

In The Hilton Memorial Garden

The garden is in motion all night
I've checked at 2.30, 4.00, and through the watches,
the agapanthus hovers, the sycamores bow.

Even in the dead of night light changes on the water
the decayed arch leans into further darkness,
the garden floods the house and I breathe Atlantic air.

The storm comes off the sea thrashing the land,
and you across the table, where are you from?
Where did you gather those looks Melanie?

The agapanthus hovers, the sycamores bow,
granite hedges and compact fields make dark divisions
under a vaulted sky – where are you from?

In the hollow night there's a spotted man flailing,
two monkeys in love, a grinning dog astride the sun
and a tipsy boat heading out below a snake horizon.

At some point, he says, I lost the liberty of words,
once it was tethered to the things of the world,
events, chemistry, the white road in the night.

I fell through a hole in the continual score,
hear me said the music before the music
in the echo landscape unvisited.

Nothing can be said of that music,
a garden, a stream of light, a coastline,
poetry only follows trailing pale ghost metaphor.

Over the hedge in the dispossessed field
I hear unseen animals breathe under stars,
set me free you cyphers for the rising descant.

Having A Drink With Phil
Kunst, Traditie En Kwaliteit

Gebruiksaanwijzing der lyriek
Lyrical Poetry: Directions for Use

*

Walking Don Van Vliet down Avenue Orban makes for a long road,
he's not easy company; leaping hedges, grinning at the Lego houses,
singing black ink mathematics into the sky as night comes down.

Bright capsules of everyone I've known glide by on grassy tracks
packed off to a different future, the girls wave wave and stroke their hair
shushed into the rolling darkness on route 39, *Come out tonight*, sings
Don.

In the black and white day night city I walk on and wait
in a moment of the Belgian Xylographic Renaissance,
the action freezes, the flags, the crowd, the girls stroking their hair.

Captain of Streetlights, Captain of Stars, give me a break;
I may as well implore you as another, Jesus Christ, my dead parents,
Paul Van Ostaijen, send me your directions for use of the lyric.

*

Leopold mounts his giant tricycle
pedals hard against the future
his white beard flaps like a fat tongue
- *Oh where is my little Caroline?*

*

'We all on earth have a commission to protect the weak from the strong.'

The king expelled us from the palace,
we left under chandeliers, exquisite taxidermy
through torture gardens and the human zoo Tervuren
saw the locals throw bananas at the exhibits in their pens.

We saw the Congolese paddle across the lakes
the park and lakes built in imitation of Versailles,
the World's Fair showcase around the colonial palace
and Expo 58, Kongorama under the Atomium.

Casement was standing off under the trees,
beard aglint, arms around his Congo Report;
I questioned the chief of the inner station
I met Conrad in Matadi, we talked through the night.

Our music - insects pinging off the iron roof,
our prospect – the trade of the dark river;
'He could tell you things. Things I have tried to forget.' said Conrad.
'We all on earth have a commission.' Casement replied.

*

Setting out for the Leopold Quarter I know the passengers,
all our heads sway together taking the bend on Orban;
Lee the inspector checks my ticket passing Mallaerts Ponds.

When do we get there? – *Well, completion, I'm not keen,* Lee says.
The monochromatic city leans in, trees stripped, human scale shot,
St. Michael casts down the rebel angels on Cinquantenaire.

They caper and preen on the arch between two worlds;
we're bound for the always open Pavilion of Human Passions
for picnic tables and playgrounds, the wrong lesson in history.

Every day heavy objects and light move freely through the city,
some resemble ideas, others not, occasionally there's a collision,
our tram broadsides a car, the flow stops, then restarts at volume.

All this activity looks precise but it's not, at the point of stasis
it starts up again each morning, in other accounts like a dream,
the heads sway together, the ghost conductor, an explosion.

*

Leaving the gig we saw families bed down for the night,
parents, three infants, eyes over the edge of the blankets;
we walked through the new development of Bourse,
the smart pedestrianisation and shiny names of Bourse.

We saw Frans Masereel let the woodcut drawing
emerge from the cutting material itself;
the material is the city, the material is us, those children,
and night came down to blacken the page.

Leaving the gig we saw the apodictic principles of poetry,
Aristotle and Van Ostaijen stood-by and pointed;
self-evident the vision the city affords, deep resonance and none,
we walked through the homeland of perfect knowledge.

*

The tram bound for Aporia passes,
driver Beckett gleams the Beckett gleam
lighting the track with his Angelus ding ding;
the routes are many and unpredictable.

Forget what Magritte would have you think,
the citizens of Brussels do not float in the sky,
they alight at random stops unsurprised
to live with unknown families for the night.

Beckett nods, waits for the green light click,
- *I repeat, I've sentences to hammer out,*
motley background static to channel,
the accounts of love to close at the terminus.

*

> *'It is at once chaotic and vague, bloated and pretentious, pompous*
> *and empty.' L'Art Moderne 1890*

So we set out for Le Pavillon des Passions Humaines in the fair May time,
the temple stands in Cinquantenaire Park close-by the Commission,
and there we found much writhing in marble though frozen in the act.

Owned at one time by King Faisal, along with the Grand Mosque;
we suffered Seduction Suicide Debauchery and Bacchanal in a pretty row,
closing at 4.45 in the summer, though how you enter is never apparent.

The 96 metre square bas-relief has a moral framework, of sorts;
the pleasures and sins overseen by Death, the Graces off to the side,
male and female principles meeting somewhere in the middle.

We arrived at the Pavilion of Human Passions in opening time,
the doors were locked and we sank to our knees at the peephole,
the interior glowed sepulchral and a cool draught stroked our faces.

In the park the trees blossomed massively and children scooted everywhere.

*

Phil, what are we talking about?
Novels. Empire. Beer. Gigs.
Instructions for the lyric.
Tram routes and Leopold.
The World's Fair of 1897.
The living and the dead.
The seven graves of Tervuren.
The full spectrum pavilion.

The Seven Graves of Tervuren

Leopold mounts his giant tricycle
his white beard flapping like a fat tongue,
pedals hard around the graves of Tervuren
gliding pneumatic on Congolese rubber.

Ekia, Gamba, Kitoukwa, M'Peia, Sambo,
Zao and Mibange, remain barely legible;
dumped in unconsecrated ground
their funeral procession booed.

For the World's Fair of 1897
in the model villages of the palace
these human exhibits died
costumed for the crowd.

Reburied in a row against the church wall
seven slabs lie at the side of the path;
we stood there and heard nothing - and heard
a song called A History of the World.

SEEING THE CITY

Tower cranes conceptualise the city,
as if swung steel and indecipherable script
articulated a theory of how it all came about
in a silver clattering language of the sky.

At the end of the working day, the golden hour,
a soft burr rises to the man in the lit cabin;
he sees the vulnerable network, various objects moving,
the configured pulse of light pause and ignite.

Then the moon is full flooding the gardens
a Masereel page empty of people,
the air still and the night more animal
settles about the darkened houses.

*

(Frans Masereel, The City)

A man with his back to us looks at the monochromatic city.
We see what he sees, no other view is presented;
industrial smoke drifts in one direction, a banner to the future.

By his density he appears superimposed on the scene,
at a distance he sees an abstract beauty to the tall city,
though clearly we are meant to have doubts about its promise.

Trains come and go at the station, blossoming more white smoke,
people come and go for the trains, gather in groups, pause mechanical,
then go about their business rather than admire the abstract beauty.

They diverge from one another until they see a fallen man;
only united by inaction, useless they stop and stare, do nothing.
History unfolds from here; in manic action, crowded isolation.

*

As if from the high cabin of a tower crane
Bruegel depicts a panorama of indifference;
floodlights, the world's traffic, a field of gibbets,
the charged circuit as ethical index unrefined.

An encyclopaedic composition is mapped;
pigs run loose in the wheat, *near het leven*
the wedding dance stamps on, children play,
a pedantic army advances in casual slaughter.

Mute mute the round mouths and blank faces,
a father holds his fingers to his child's mouth,
- *Hungry monsieur, hungry,*
bedded down outside the Bruegel show.

*

On Grand Champ across a square of gardens
I saw a Chinese ideogram crash from the sky,
the watercolour clouds of *Shou* lit by halogen charisma.

In another script a lopsided lower case *t* cuts an angle,
the horizontal extended brings it down to earth
gantries and ladders barely visible in the gloom.

A culture swings into place over the houses of the living;
in the delicacy of this engineering a city thrives, sings
packages of products and services for the home market.

If I climbed, strut by strut, in bare feet, eyes open,
up through the steel rib tunnel in high-vis orange
and hopped along the jib with plural flightpath birds,

tasting iron on my tongue, head lost in weather systems,
I would more keenly see the beauty laid out at night,
the spiralling lights and the fixed, the river of traffic, the fall.

John Berryman Played the Accordion

There was a choir later that night
alive the many voices anonymous.

John Berryman, grinning, played the accordion
approximately, something broken from youth.

Put the *Schlager* back in the box, John Berryman said,
I stand for difficulty, disclosure, rage.

Next time around I'll take up the accordion, he said,
his genius for accelerated feeling restored.

*

(For Sara Evans and Damien Papin)

Later there were musicians in the street,
a young man, a young woman with mandolin and harp.

As if at first only imagined and unplaced,
morceaux traditionnels from many parts of Europe.

The song held the air and hovered in doorways
making a pause in terrestrial motion.

We walked to find the origin of the music within reach
and night came down gently like the end of time.

*

There are occasions in the world restored to precise experience
that perhaps were never there in the first place.

Though everything of saying says look, here at hand,
you can walk into the centre of the shape made by the sound.

There was a dark horizon of mountains across the water
and I heard the first song broadcast on Radio Apollon.

The ferry had left and there was nowhere else to go
and the waves ran under the quay in exact measure.

THE BONES OF THEM ARE KEEPING

We climbed the calderimi, Taygetos above,
let a yellow dog run and looked out for snakes,
the sea a bowl of light we're heading for.

Across the square in Agios Dimitrios a mulberry tree
catches the sunlight in its spreading branches
as if the light pours from the sprouting leaves.

Give me your unfurling hand, I would take your hand
in that dance, the opposite of dying,
as the vetch and daisies rise in a wave.

The sky opens to magnify the earth incandescent,
the sun a path of broken glass to the other shore,
a radiant scatter cast this way.

*

'Just beside, there is the Catholic church with the friends of Greece
monument. In the crypt, the bones of them are keeping. Lord Byron
was a real friend of this country. This is the reason we called our
hostelry by his name.'

*

Tonight a crowd fills the square in Nafplio for Good Friday,
the bower of white and purple flowers for Jesus held aloft
and purple banners for Jesus hanging from high windows;
priests, acolytes and bigwigs on stage but not a girl up there.

The silver band plays in death-march to lead the parade,
kyrie eleison
and there's a baby in pink rabbit costume on my shoulder,
kyrie eleison
and for one moment everyone stops talking
kyrie eleison
and the shops dim their lights for the parade to pass.

Let me join those families, lose me in that crowd,
the children grasp the strings of their ascendant balloons
the cartoon faces nod and genuflect above us all;
Ky rie e leis ON with a thump on the big drum.

LISTENING TO COUNTRY MUSIC

I'm sending you this from Agios Dimitrios,
October light on the sea as summer retreats,
the days strung out like amber beads of the turning world;
we can walk along the shore and see its radiance dissolve.

I can no more describe the light than walk on water
I hold everything, I hold nothing:
but on sighting the sea we shout Thalassa Thalassa
for the great enterprise; catastrophe tops the brim.

St. Dimitrios lives above the harbour they say,
I hear their singing, their octosyllabic miroloyia,
another lit photograph fixed to a headstone,
another grave to feed and water and talk to.

And the rain will be good for the olives,
straight-down spears of light falling on our heads,
the sound of its descent rising like inescapable thought
buoys us up in the layered distance of the mountains.

The island off shore is no bigger than a big rock,
there you find the bronze statues of the Discouri
standing a foot high in the open air of Pephnos,
the sea sweeps over in winter and never moves them.

A sparrow's two-tone chatter elevates the blue dome
over Taygetos and the gulf, the distance unimaginable.

*

I don't get Apollo, the far-seeing flash youth
but we were drunk listening to country music
attendant upon the god using women for target practice
and Jason Isbell sang – *she smelt of cigarettes and wine*
flitting back to Delphi in the blink of Spring.

The mist rolls in off the sea, leave the door open tonight,
Apollo the village boy walks out by the shore unencumbered,
- I've stopped thinking of the Indo-European question, he said,
of John Berryman's whiskey tears.
I'm Apollo, look, I'll show you my head full of light,
the human catalogue of irresistible actions,
lyres, vulvas, arrows in flight, ravens made black.

*

There's no account of Euripides' trek north to Macedon
slogging through The Valley of Tempe to voluntary exile,
writing The Bacchae on a tangent to Athenian reason;
snow-blind, snowbound, Euripides evokes the stranger god.

Dionysus steps forward and announces himself,
I am, lisping, eyes of kohl shine insouciant liquefaction,
I am . . . is how a god would enter your life;
a figure of concealed and absolute concentration.

Here's a box of Bacchant tricks and fireworks,
fawn skin, thyrsus, bottle of beer, dancing shoes.
Sweet fool, my toys burn holes in your piddling days.
If I landed my radiant gaze would melt your bones.

What do you imagine you have apart from me?
Think back, at first you knew what? There you go,
an alert body, hungry, ready to eat the whole world,
a figure of concealed and absolute concentration.

*

(For musicians Sam Bailey and Jack Hues)

Down here below the glass of waves
I hear no music, no chordal tides,
no Brad Mehldau, no Christian Scott.

Jack, Jack – can you hear me?
Sam, my ears are full of the turning sea;
for just one song I would come back.

I would come back and walk down your street
of foolish things, of Sam at the piano
playing the whole world open-eyed.

Jack pitch an opera at the lowering sky
sound out the tones to change the climate,
let the music play us like swimming.

*

Nina Simone lived in the Republic of Song,
she married there several times and on occasion was happy;
once she arrived in the Republic from Montreux 1976.

Her earliest point of entry was that first recital
in the library Tryon, North Carolina, at ten years old
to raise money to continue her musical training.

She refused to play until her parents were restored to the front row.
Daddy you can do what you like but I won't play until;
years later, I sing from intelligence, said Nina Simone.

*

Sam Plays Sam Speaks

A mythology of playing and speaking
I said from my mouth from my fingers.

From my mouth from my fingers
to beat the logos out of thinking.

Sam said from the tipping edge of thought
I don't know what I'm saying Sam said.

Why bother with the prefabricated
any fool can fill bloated museums.

*(Sam now say 6 things that come to your mind, tell me and I'll write
them back to you. Perhaps you include even the present statement).*

1

2

3

4

5

6

My life as a DJ didn't work out.

Why taunt the dumb beast?

First broadcast of the day.

To beat the logos out of speaking.

Back to the stream of first meaning.

From the mouths of all the people.

*

There's a single point of light on the mountain,
the air between here and there is a substance, an intoxication.
I know the village, the steep road, the houses rising in terraces;
there's music there tonight, two sinuous old men singing
throw the economy on the fire – we all know these songs, always have.

We sing up and the year rolls forward against the odds;
by such means springs erupt, the wind drinks pine tree resin
and the sweep of the valley presents a map of itself.
A boy steps forward to dance before his family,
the faltering 9/4 measure jigs the Zeibekiko bones.

Subterranean the music tilts the calderimi to the sea,
disintegrates the squared stones of the village walls,
breaks our contracts rattling bolts in the night
and makes us beasts clamour and dream,
monosyllabic and simple on the chambered ground.

*

If you are a big tree I am a small axe sings Orpheus
his lyre cocked – and carved from the tree addressed,
strings of air stretched and tuned to magical numbers,
a question of long division and sweet intervals.

If I'm what? said the tree, panicking the whole forest,
a single wave of sound crashing mountains, valleys, cities.
The ratio of matter anti-matter means something said Orpheus,
1: 10,000,000,000 for instance means the world's congealed song.

Ughh, the mass of it, gibbering, unformed, the anti-poem;
that's why I have to chop some life into it, right into the grain.
It's not easy, you try it, harvesting by acoustics only;
my voice, my juice right into it, notch by notch, note by note.

*

There is another version of Orpheus going to hell for Eurydice. In this
other version Orpheus must not say Eurydice's name because this,
rather than turning to see if she is following him, will abandon her to
that no place of shadows. He must not even shape the sound of her
name.

It could be represented like this:

must not speak
walk she follows
must not speak
you rid he see
you you you rid
rid see sea seed.

Eurydice Eurydice Eurydice
her hand on my shoulder
its warmth lighter than
and then turning gone
in song set hell spinning.

It could be represented like this:
I know the name I say in darkness.

I hold everything, I hold nothing;
the distance unimaginable.

A Revision of Jack Spicers's Helen: A Revision

Everything is known about Helen but her voice,
setting fires as a history of conflagration in the culture
even over the icy sea echoing in your ear,
even further north over the white shelf of falling.

For history I went to the North Pole Helen,
the magnetic music sought us out, made us naked;
it was nothing like a vision, just orders from above.
For history I went to the North Pole Helen.

Daddy Zeus President was there, squalling and whining;
he feared Helen was on her way,
he feared he did not exist, blah blah blah;
most of us wished that was the case.

His voice is like that because the sky enfolds him:
the sky, contrails, flight paths, satellites – is boss.
They are not signs but items in the big emporium,
and below he drills holes in the fourth wall for immunity.

I won't do the ghost walk pelted with soft fruit, he said.
On the battlefield with the real dead of the new old world
you can choose to name the smashed up plants and people
but know there's a simple opera rolling in the grass.

Finally Helen was in transit, her make-up sent on to Egypt.
There are particular insects in the desert, to be kept from the eyes;
Helen's eyes brighter than bright dehydrated the heart,
no artifact could do this, her presence runs in the nerves.

In your name my love I break off to write to you,
the space between us a matter of low resistance parabasis.
I can imagine you in Egypt, in Troy but not returning,
after much slaughter, to down-home Sparti.

If we harvest black ghosts starvation follows,
seeds of dust smeared on the faces of friends,
dumb and unable to grasp their own interest;
reckless love 754 miles off, from Sparti to Troy.

You must go there to set the poem aside.
They know everything about Helen there.

THE PLEATS OF THE SUN

We were in the air listening to the song about Icarus
holding the silver thread of morning like a tune,
turbulence flipped the flight attendant over on all fours.
Icarus thought it funny until he touched the silver thread;
fizzing in the air like a firework, his first and last sunrise,
he saw a picture of the world turning and forgetting.

The olive trees swayed as one, clapped their little hands,
- *There's no conspiracy on Earth,* Aeolis said, *just gravity,*
but given what you know about human nature . . .
We fell towards the sea, assumed the diving position,
the blue and grey perfection suddenly less abstract;
the captain sang the song about Icarus over and over.

*

I sit in the last corner of courtyard sunlight,
see the shadow plot diurnal, clouds resist quotation
drifting high across the shadowed mountains.

We step, we talk according to Homeric measure,
it's a matter of time gone deep, uncounted;
we've been inventing this song for generations.

My neighbours gather in the olive groves and high meadows,
bodies passing seen in the intervals of leaves,
I mean, they seem like drifting confetti of light.

Nothing is more beautiful than this temporary coruscation,
the refrain, the pause for thought, the contact made;
it secures nothing but sings the epic of a shared breath.

*

The roadside kafaneio is a stage-set lit by a summer morning.
Old men sit off to the side in the shade for a first drink. Variously
garlanded figures assemble. Working men before work pull up for a
coffee and a smoke. The young women, made-up, hair done, dressed
ready, run the place, tease and serve. The backdrop through the big
windows behind the counter is a huge sweep of sea fit to break your
heart like a world of endless blue, endless promise. The men load up,
come and go. The women attend and smile.
- *Maria you are as fresh as morning.*
- *What do you want Petro?* And tickles the palm of his extended hand.
- *What I want is a break, and you.*

*

'the terrace is full
of salty murmurs
the dress and even
the pleats of the sun'

(Chanson Dada, Tristan Tzara, translated Lee Harwood.)

The days are columns of light
let them go in the unexplored grove
to stand apparent in the open air
an unfixed cartography surrounds them.

Those voyages unforgotten as bright shards
scattered trace another coast
after the submerged marble gardens
comes the first smell of the land.

Leaving the house I'm caught
that moment of evening, the wind in the pine,
the colour shift of earth, bronze mountains.
Lee, that moment you would know.

THE
MUSEUM
OF
THE SEA

The Museum of the Sea

Setting out, the sun a risen fire
launched a day of promise
set to breakers
cutting the wave of the unknown.

1 Morning

He cut the motor at the exact point to glide and
slot the boat in place in one continuous movement
rope slung and tied stepped from deck to quay
six strides to the moped, one kick, turnover and gone.

An art accomplished for a box of small fry, unseen by tourists;
of the sea, of the harbour, made invisible to them,
lethargic in sports casuals seeking the real, the photogenic.
What you want today? How much? Υεια σας κύριε. Look what I got.

Transparent he moved across the light
rolling from deep time over the harbour wall,
just going about his business, occupied;
the world of gods, the porch of ghosts, Ithaca of rock.

I watch the boats come and go, the spare catch
splashed silver on zinc tables splinter morning;
- How much you pay me today? What you want today?
- Look what I got. Sardeles. Gavros. Gopas.

I want the fleets of Pharis, Sparta, Messe to return
the friends of former days to come by,
to see that company, night on their shoulders
stepping over the harbour wall into yellow light.

The face absent at the table gone to remittance work,
to Europe and the America, the commerce
of the first ports lost like thought in a salt medium,
the spark they struck burning in a dark sea.

That year, land-blown, they took to the ships,
some from poverty, others from chemical fire;
to find the poor season, the thin time of strawmen,
to find a clue, a song in a village adrift by the sea:

Little red queen, little red queen seated in her barge,
smacked-mouth lips and curly crown aglow;
attendants dip and bow, display their scarlet values,
their hearts and their vulvas like pretty purple roses.

And it was the same loading, the same departure,
by generation, processional of those taken,
all the traffic of the lives of men and women
bound in the trailing waves of abduction.

I watch the boats come, I watch the boats go; out there,
at the point of failing vision, the day shows promise
and the world turns for a line of light to advance
reaching to the absent and talk of the work in hand.

Little red queen, little red queen
your attendants dip and bow.

They sailed the upper sea of the setting sun,
for the pebble cut to resemble a woman
250,000 years ago at Berekhat Ram;
I would hold her in my hand.

Little red queen, little red queen.

2 Setting Out

The ladder into the sea made of rusted alloy
shifts with each step taken,
rung by rung the body submerges
surrounded by the rising coolness of time.

Keep to the left leaving the harbour
see the water pales in the shallows,
a fatal turquoise surrounds us, slow slow,
the wind's almost absent.

In an ABS plastic shell of 158 kilograms
afloat on a sea 4 miles down,
the silence deep enough overwhelms talk,
the village quit from sight, faces forgotten.

Go low on the water to find acceptance,
to find where the fresh water streams emerge,
swim in the cold eye of the sea
the still ellipses glassy on the surface.

Only the slow accumulation of detail
will keep you safe, keep you above the waves,
will have you come back one day, just to see
if you're remembered by the village girls.

Say goodbye to the bar for the glassy-eyed
the taverna for the lost,
the strophe anti-strophe of a comedy
called Sunseeker Self-Congratulation.

The light breaks in a line advancing
and with morning the point stands clear
away from the business of the land
the white surfaces rise and fall aside.

You can swim into the caves of Kato Figi
and all the acoustic caves of the sea,
at any turn sink below the rising truth
sound the shape of descent in pretty song.

Swifts dart indifferent into the blue,
emit a net of signals scored in air;
we crawl under roots, over copper streams,
deeper into snake-dark, air-still silence.

Descend through words, pictures, obliteration
below white dots punched in grey rock
picturing a pistol like a diving dolphin;
the war continues and the earth makes no answer.

P. Pterneas
A. Strateas
A. Manoleas
S. Christeas
Panayotis Petreas

and above 1881
and above 2-8-43
       1946
and above
the war makes another war
blue on ochre stained
the rising coolness of time.

  *

As if from nowhere, there was lapis lazuli,
stone splashed with water shone brightest blue.
Lapis lazuli, the mouth saying it, – from where?
And you the lapis lazuli girl in your estate.

Even the name unknown until then,
lapis lazuli goddess you processed.
It was as if everything, the whole world
fell into the arms of the harbour.

Seventy miles by sea took a day and night,
a day and night to shrink the world to market:
obsidian, seashell, carved chlorite bowls,
bitumen – to stick together the bricks of Babylon.

Obsidian, good for butchery, good for war,
good for scarification and shaping marble;
pots decorated, their temples teeming,
a riot of boats, vulvas, fish and stars.

Out from the islands the captains came,
gliding over a sea of gods, raiding the divine,
opening the sea-lanes to the unknown.
Shamash – comfort us at sea, let us not fear the waves.

They say she gave birth to a bull,
they were the people of the goddess
and the host sat around in a circle,
and the goddess gave birth to a bull.

Weapons, tools and jewellery
items for trade, diplomacy and war
from 7 different countries, empires and states,
for beauty and for slaughter.

3 Trade

Nation by nation they fall upon the meadows of Asia;
ships the hardware, dictated by the muses – listen,
so packed their oars clattering sing on the water
the men, strung flesh only, febrile, a horde.

And you mean to set this lot against that city?
Boiotians 50 ships, Minyans 30, Phokians 40.
It goes on and on, nation by nation they come;
I make this 1,186 ships, I make this unthinkable.

Odysseus and his Ithacans only 30 ships
grinning dogs for the most part
the man a fleet of cunning on his own,
the whispering self of many selves, twisting.

If anyone wants an account I'll give it,
wine dark vile sea swallowed us
the waves fucked us every way up,
delivered us to one hole or another.

Sucking the beauty out of slaughter
I lost my taste for the tang of the ditch,
old men and young men scattered like trash
on the altar of the plain.

Smoke ascending in endless blue - futile,
blood descending in the purple fosse,
just limbs, organs, offal - futile
nation by nation they fall.

Down the no-return tunnel from the west,
we lay down on the meadows of Asia
dreamt a war and a return nation by nation;
noise travelling over water to silence.

*

So they come and go at the water's edge
site a bearing, mark by mark choose a course
that headland say, then set out across rolling blank,
recalling the sound of a remark barely heard.

Ghosted periplus of a nameless land drawn,
unrecorded on any chart, the captain's book;
and at every turn to contend with sweet *himeros,*
the way that track climbs the remembered hill.

Well you best forget most everything else,
it might do boys, once harvesting the sea begins
and you've taken the spoil of others,
but forget the land that only rarely tilted.

*

I sit and see it all, they come and go, the living the dead;
I sit because I can't do anything else, shipped-up, caked in salt,
against this harbour wall, white-wash lifting, pock-marked,
you wouldn't see me if I didn't move, and I don't much.

I remember a morning we set out in the black ships,
I remember her face, how she turned and spoke – and the light.
What I see is vision, I mean it's there, and below the water too
but the ground is uncertain with items unretrieved.

Those the things recalled before the final deal
the objects made subject to aqueous corrosion,
how she stood in the doorway, the garden floating
and how the turning world came sailing in.

The harbour opens to the little sea-gates of memory
but thought on that tide is borne at a cost, then washed away.
I see everything as on a screen, though the surface is unfixed,
my eyes transparent from seeing – and what's the use of that?

Then as now, the tide washed over, and I'm as glass under water;
my thallasocracy at my feet, a snapped oar, frayed rope, an empty tin.
Salute the king of sea rubbish, sea scrap, the ships unreturned,
the big fish eaten by little fish, their bones picked clean on the seabed.

My absolute vision runs on the waves, here's an account if you like;
ships – burning towers – a woman. Enough? Add this: the war
continues.
I remember a morning when those black ships set out
leaving a white trail sparkling to the edge of the known.

And falling over that horizon, a single boat makes easy passage
under cover from Marathonisi through the museum of the sea.

4 Drowning

'Set sail without fear, for though I lost myself to the sea, others who
sailed the same day put safely into harbour.'

No-one takes to the sea lightly,
you starve or sail or both,
so farewell my little ones.
There's no music sad enough.

350 copper ingots (10 tons)
1 ton of tin, thus 11 tons of bronze

We couldn't make sheltered water,
the sound of cliff-wash faded;
smell of thyme, fennel on the air
from the land we couldn't reach.

1 metric ton of terebinth resin
2 dozen ebony logs from Nubia

Himeros
If you sail beyond Cape Malea
forget your homeland
there's no return   *Himeros.*

In time we're all bound
for the heartless body of water,
washed-up, washed-out, bleached bones.
There's no music then.

200 ingots of raw glass from Mesopotamia
dark blue, light blue, purple, honey and amber

Under the breaking wave
white borne on the blue
beauty steps ashore.
There's no music sad enough.

pottery from Cyprus and Caanan, oil lamps,
bowls, jugs, jars, scarabs and cylinder seals

*

At night lights low on the water set out in darkness,
three lights, a one-man fishing boat, a living;
and elsewhere on the other side of the same small sea.

Pity those who take the 25 minute crossing,
pity those who make it and those who don't,
25 minutes, $1,500 sailing into darkness.

swords, daggers from Italy and Greece
a stone sceptre-mace from the Balkans

Spring of everything rising from the earth
Spring of everything drowning in sight of land
the air a chamber of birdsong wide as the sky.

*   *24 stone anchors*

We all went sucked into the salt mouth
not at the sea gates in blue light running,
nor dancing the bow wave whisper;
the sleeping stone cast and never retrieved.

A fouled hull scours the soft flesh
the face, the genitals and suchlike,
the water's red but no memory remains,
below a blue ellipse closing.

14 pieces of hippopotamus ivory, 1 elephant tusk
statue of Canaanite deity, bronze overlaid in gold

We suffered the vision of closest things
everything drowned to support bees,
to house the pretty sea slug, the lichen spirals,
the crab waiting to loosen our sinews.

*remains of grapes, pomegranates, figs,
coriander, sumac and other spices*

*

His name was Alan Kurdi
a small body in the water
he was three years old.

*gold jewellery, pendants, a gold chalice,
duck-shaped ivory cosmetic containers*

Out of the arms of his mother
out of the arms of his father
they will never hold him again.

Out of the arms of his mother
out of the arms of his father
they will never smell him again.

*a yellow baseball cap, a black headscarf
a map of Europe, two rucksacks*

*

We sang hymns
to Lord Wethead
Sir Teeming Waters
King Rolling Waves
God Streaming Locks
himself Poseidon
but he's a mean cunt.

Comfort yourself
sail without fear
the Great Green Sea
the Sea of Joppa

the Middle Sea
the White Sea
churning hope.

Press on press on
without fear
the Lampedusa route
the Lesbos route.
Make ready a riot
a flood a troop
nation by nation.

*

From seven countries, empires and states
weapons, tools and jewellery,
items for trade, diplomacy and war,
for a vision of furthest things.

Bejewel my hand, armour my heart
for beauty and for slaughter,
drop the world at my door
and set in gold its raw taste.

5 Let's Leave

What you want today? Look what I got.
Out of the big sea I had this thought, OK,
stranger, out of the big sea turning backward.
Do you think my hands don't tell the story?
Do you think I've not always been here?

You see there's an Ithaca and a wife
the pleasure of my eyes and hands,
out there somewhere in the echo-scape
before I took to the dealings of the world
before the pull of this island or another.

The sea's roar will drill a hole in your head
and leave you with nothing, companions lost,
memory shot, what you have is what you catch
and what you will see you will see in one light
and at the end there's a clearing, held then gone.

Tell the rhapsode sing or else, tell the rhapsode,
song the only harbour to gain at the close;
I see my island, up from the port to my house
this path I know, these white rocks I know
and the sea all around a vertiginous blue of air.

On all fours in the waves I remembered
I dreamt I was climbing that path, that other story
of the trick of my return, Telemachus, Penelope;
and I dreamt the great restoration,
that the ground might quit rolling under my feet.

I might stop here, scoop a handful of earth.
Look, they said, look at that old man crawling,
he's piss wet, he looks like a dog.
Where the hell's he come from?
Look at him burrow in the ground.

I tell you, if Helen was an appearance on the walls
a seeming woman, ghost queen of the bloody plane,
then I never returned, Ithaca a name only,
the slaughter futile and nothing
and nothing the going out and return.

*

Little red queen, little red queen,
we sing for you far off - What you want today?
Did we serve you true? Launch your boat aright?
Do you hold us in your heart?
Little red queen, little red queen, riding on the sea.

What is it that we do as the sky darkens
and talk submits to the slow sound of the sea?
A nocturnal hierarchy returns, a bat flits a signal
an old woman talks kindly to a dog,
and owls weave mortal wires into dawn.

Night falls and the bronze hills turn pink,
a fishing boat sets out against the odds
outboard drones a bow wave whisper,
the moon rises over cloud above Taygetos
making a terrestrial bed of light.

Village voices engulfed drift to an ending,
the harbour wall retains the heat of a long history;
radiant click of Ares, the honey of Helen's mouth;
the sea is dark, the night is dark, we are free,
the boat's there, sits easy on the water, let's leave.

ACKNOWLEDGMENTS

Several of the poems in *To Write a Mythology* have appeared in earlier versions; ARTICLE 50, Longbarrow Press 2018. TWITTERS FOR A LARK: POETRY OF THE EUROPEAN UNION OF IMAGINARY WRITERS, as Eua Ionnu, Shearsman, 2017. My thanks go to Brian Lewis and Robert Sheppard.

Earlier versions of 'The White Road' and 'Messages Coming In' were first published in the chapbook BELOW THIS LEVEL, 2019.

'The Sinking Colony Revisited in the Days of Lee Harwood.' Began life in WINTERREISEN a collaboration with Alan Halsey, published by Knives Forks and Spoons. Although these are my parts from the collaborative poem much is owed to Alan. I'm also grateful to him for the title of the poem and his naming of the figure Iain Guido Smith.

Several poems from *The Republic of Song* were published in The Fortnightly Review with thanks to the editor Peter Riley. 'Grahamland' was first published in THE CAUGHT HABITS OF LANGUAGE, Donut Press, 2018, edited by Rachael Boast, Andy Ching and Nathan Hamilton.

The poem for Roy Fisher (1930-2017) first appeared in Molly Bloom edited by Aidan Semmens. An earlier version of 'I'm sending you this from Agios Dimitrios' for Denise Riley was published in THE WORLD SPEAKING BACK, Boiler House Press, 2018, edited by Ágnes Lehóczky and Zoë Skoulding. My thanks go to all of these editors.

NOTES

Radio Logos part 2. 'There is no history that does not relate to the present,' Louis Gernet quoted in THE MEDITERRANEAN IN THE ANCIENT WORLD, Fernand Braudel, 2002.

The Sinking Colony Revisited in the Days of Lee Harwood. See THE SINKING COLONY, 1970, Lee Harwood 1939-2015.

Come Up Come Up. A HISTORY OF THE WORLD IN TWELVE MAPS, Jerry Brotton, 2014.

Roy Fisher, 1930-2017, 'zig-zagging like the shadow of a hare', from *Wonders of Obligation.*

Grahamland. The line 'Launched even later there becoming a time.' is culled from THE SEVEN JOURNEYS, W S Graham, 1944, and takes the first word from the first line of each of the seven poems, more or less.

BN. Ben Nicholson, 1894-1982. See BEN NICHOLSON: 'chasing out something alive' drawings and painted reliefs 1950-75, Peter Khoroche, 2002.

In The Hilton Memorial Garden. Roger Hilton, 1911-1975, painter.

Having a Drink with Phil. The essay *Lyrical Poetry: Directions for Use* by Paul Van Ostaijen can be found in THE FIRST BOOK OF SCHMOLL, Paul Van Ostaijen translated by Theo Hermans, James S. Holmes and Peter Nijmeijer, 2015. The phrase, 'the homeland of perfect knowledge' is from that essay. For material relating to Roger Casement, Joseph Conrad and Leopold II see KING LEOPOLD'S GHOST, Adam Hochschild, 2006; ROGER CASEMENT, Brian Inglis, 1973; THE KING INCORPORATED, Neal Ascherson, 1963 and THE EYES OF ANOTHER RACE: Roger Casement's Congo Report and 1903 Diary, edited by Séamas Ó Síocháin and Michael O'Sullivan, 2003.

Listening to Country Music. The Jason Isbell song quoted is *Cigarettes and Wine* from *Jason Isbell And The 400 Unit.*

'If you are a big tree, I am a small axe'. *Small Axe* written by Bob Marley, sung by U Roy.

Helen: A Revision. Jack Spicer in MY VOCABULARY DID THIS TO ME: THE COLLECTED POETRY OF JACK SPICER, edited by Peter Gizzi and Kevin Killian, 2008.

The Museum of the Sea. For, 'Set sail without fear . . .' Theodorides quoted in THE MAKING OF THE MIDDLE SEA, Cyprian Broodbank, 2013.

About the Author

Kelvin Corcoran lives in Brussels. His most recent work includes *Facing West*, 2017, the Medicine Unboxed sponsored *Not Much to Say Really*, 2017, *Article 50*, 2018 and *Below This Level*, 2019. The sequence 'Helen Mania' was a Poetry Book Society choice and the poem 'At the Hospital Doors' was highly commended by the Forward Prize jury 2017. His work is the subject of a study edited by Professor Andy Brown, *The Poetry Occurs as Song*, 2013. He has edited an account of the poetry of Lee Harwood in *Not the Full Story: Six Interviews with Lee Harwood*, 2008.

In addition, his poetry has been commissioned to accompany Arts Council exhibitions of British modernist art. He has collaborated with various musicians and composers both in performance and recording, producing the CD *A Thesis on the Ballad* with The Jack Hues Quartet. His work has been anthologised in the UK and the USA and translated into Greek and Spanish. He is the guest editor of the *Shearsman* poetry magazine.

Photograph of the author by Melanie Warnes. Used by permission.

www.ingramcontent.com/pod-product-compliance
Lightning Source LLC
Chambersburg PA
CBHW022039090426
42741CB00007B/1124